To Lynne!
Thank you for your
support. I'm grateful
for your support,
friendship, you'll
I'll always have
back no matter

BE YOUR OWN COLLEGE ADVISOR

Your money management guide into and through college

Dr. Crystal R. Hudson, Ph.D.

Dr. Crystal R. Hudson

TABLES OF CONTENT

ACKNOWLEDGEMENT

This book is my way of giving back to others because of all the blessings I've received. Maybe this book will help someone who is thinking about going to college and investing in themselves. First and foremost, I'd like to thank God for always being with me and always blessing me. I'd like to especially thank him for my family who have always loved, supported, and encouraged me. I'm thankful for my village, which was led by my mother, Mrs. Velma Harris and my grandmother, Mrs. Alice Austin, who nurtured and raised me into the person I am today. I'm thankful for my siblings, Kim Sargent, Benny Hudson Jr., Andre Harris and Aaron Harris who have always been my best friends, confidants and support when I needed it. I'm also thankful for all my nieces and nephews.

Growing up I was either in school, reading a book or playing some sport. I'd like to thank all my teachers and coaches from St. Rita's Elementary School to Scecina High School. School and sports kept me out of trouble, and their example led me to become a coach and an educator. I'd also like to thank all my professors and coaches at Indiana University (IU), Clark Atlanta University (CAU), and the University of Georgia (UGA). I'd especially like to thank my professors at CAU's Business School who truly provide a family atmosphere. I am a professor today because of them.

INTRODUCTION

My prayer for you is that you experience financial freedom and never have to be stressed about money. Financial freedom, where you can easily pay your bills and have money left over to accomplish your goals whether it's to travel on a regular basis, purchase your dream home, or help friends/family members. When helping friends/family members, I take the advice of the airlines that says to put on your air mask first before helping others. In other words, once you're financially stable, help others in need.

This book is my passion because everyone deserves a great college experience without it financially ruining them or their family. Throughout the book, I give examples of those who graduated from college debt free, and without their credit being ruined before they start their careers. I understand that it is tempting to accept those large refunds, based on student loans, and tempting to apply for credit cards when you really don't have the means to pay it off each month. My advice is to just say "NO." You must be the protector of your financial life or be your own advisor while you're in college.

There's a student who runs up to me every time she sees me on the promenade and says, "Dr. Hudson, I'm going to graduate debt free." She received a scholarship that pays all her tuition due to her academic performance and she hustled and found more scholarships to pay for her housing. That's what I'm talking about. If she can do it, anyone can do it.

Chapter 1

MY STORY

I have always believed that the best investment a person can make is by obtaining a college degree. A degree provides opportunities and experiences beyond your wildest imagination. It can also be your stepping stone into a better life.

Students should also go away to college, at least an hour from home, to be independent from their parents. A college experience where you're constantly learning, debating, and growing tends to shape one's life for the better. Considering what a college education has to offer, it does not have to cost an arm and a leg, and it certainly should not put anyone deep in debt.

My college education enabled me to move beyond my small world of Indianapolis, Indiana, move into the middle class, live comfortably in multiple states, and travel throughout the world. I've also accomplished my dream career as a college professor at a HBCU (Historically Black College and University), where I can positively impact young minds.

I began my college journey at Indiana University (IU) on the Bloomington campus. Living up to my self-proclaimed title of "lifelong learner," four years after IU, I obtained an MBA in finance from Clark Atlanta University (CAU) in Atlanta, Georgia. Not only has this degree served me well in my professional career, but my experience at a HBCU was life changing. After graduating from CAU and spending fifteen years in corporate America, I went on to earn a PhD from the University of Georgia and began that dream job of being a college professor at Clark Atlanta University.

Working in higher education is perfect for me because I love being in a classroom. I've always told my family and friends, "If being a student paid better, I would have been a student for the rest of my life." I am fortunate to have found the next best thing which is being a professor on a college campus. Professors are always engaged in research of one type or another to advance the body of knowledge within their discipline. Being a part of this research community is another benefit of my professorship because it makes me feel like a student, constantly exploring and learning something new.

Also, when you're on a college campus there's always something going on. For example, in 2013, President Barack Obama delivered the commencement address at Morehouse's graduation, and I was there. We had to bear the rain to hear his inspiring speech, but it was worth it. Another example is the series of social justice marches on campuses in 1993 to protest the Rodney King beating and I was there.

I've always been able to travel abroad personally and as a professor. Recently, I led a study abroad excursion to Amsterdam, Netherlands. Most of the students we took to Amsterdam had never been outside of the country. I also took a trip to the Dominican Republic with other professors from minority universities and colleges. My next excursion will be to Italy or Africa, and I'm looking forward to it.

Where It All Started:
    I can honestly say that education changed my life. Ever since I was a student at St. Rita's Catholic School, I loved to read and loved math. St. Rita's curriculum used "Program Readers" that allowed students to read and progress at their own pace. These Program Readers introduced me to "Mythology," a genre I quickly grew to appreciate. I also looked forward to the Book Mobile visiting our school because I loved getting books like *Encyclopedia Brown* and the *Nancy Drew* series. Also, as a child I loved reading *Ritchie Rich* comic books, which is probably why I study personal finance.

    Mathematics was my second love as a child, and St. Rita's fostered that passion as well. My 7th and 8th grade math teacher allowed and encouraged students to learn at our own pace. I also participated in the Math Olympics, which further enhanced my mathematical abilities. I have heard that a child's foundation is established in 1st to 3rd grades, and I believe that's true. St. Rita's Catholic School provided that foundation for me.

My Angels:
    The Lord has blessed me with my personal angels: my mother, Velma Harris, and my grandmother, Alice M. Austin (i.e., Nanny). Both of my angels always emphasized the importance of education. Although our family really could not afford the tuition, they always found a way to pay for my siblings and I to attend St. Rita's Catholic School and later, attend Scecina Catholic High School because of their reputation for providing a premier education. We were probably the only kids living in the projects while attending private schools.

Attending private schools and being exposed to an environment at a higher social class was a brilliant way for my angels to inspire me to want more out of life. I often wonder if this was intentional. While in high school, I was a member of the National Honors Society. Every month we'd have outings to Clowes Hall to see plays like *West Side Story* and *The Sound of Music*. Nanny would buy me a new outfit for every outing. I think that was her way of saying that she was proud of me.

It was no accident that my profession and passion are in finance. I learned how to manage money by watching my grandmother. For as long as I can remember, Nanny ran the household and managed its finances. Nanny did a great job of managing and saving her money, and typically held one credit card for emergencies and special occasions. She paid off that credit card every month because she didn't like being in debt nor paying interest. When I was in high school, Nanny bought a laundromat for $6,000 cash. This was back in the 1980's and I had no idea she had that kind of money. She owned and worked at the laundromat for several years. Nanny later sold the laundromat to a dry cleaner and made a nice profit on the transaction. Her financial maneuvers taught me much of what I use today.

Focus on Free Money:
Education has been the catalyst for me to excel in life. While at IU and CAU, I hustled finding scholarships and grants to pay for my education. Even as an undergrad I knew exactly how much I needed to live on, and I didn't take more than I needed. I typically was a work study student, working at the library or for a professor. The key to earning these degrees without burying myself in debt was planning and finding various other ways to fund my college education.

Although we had an abundance of love in my family, we did not have an abundance of money to pay for college, and I understood that. Therefore, to subsidize my degree at Indiana University I first obtained an athletic scholarship and later was awarded need-based grants. In other words, free money. Similarly, I paid for my MBA at Clark Atlanta University mainly through an Executive Scholarship based on maintaining a high GPA.

From my experiences, I learned that once a student is accepted into a PhD program and is appointed to an assistantship, oftentimes, the tuition is completely waived. The assistantship usually involves working for a professor, for which the student receives a monthly stipend to help cover living expenses. My financial acumen comes from Nanny, who also made sure that everyone in the family was financially okay.

My Corporate Career:
Getting a degree from Indiana University (IU) was strategic in not only elevating me to the middle class, but also enabling me to work and live beyond my hometown of Indianapolis, IN. IU's business school is recognized worldwide, and it allowed me to work for companies such as Frito-Lay and Indiana Bell, utilizing the Operations side of my Operations & Systems Management degree. However, my desired career was within finance, so I went back to get my MBA in finance from CAU.

Clark Atlanta University's business school has always been known for producing top notch business professionals. As such, companies flock to CAU's business school in search of this talent. CAU's business school gave me that opportunity to transition into finance. So, after getting my MBA in finance and obtaining a great finance internship with Xerox, I began my finance career.

Within corporate finance, I specialized in consumer products and my talent was combining finance with technology. Coming out of CAU, I worked for Sara Lee Corporation, in the Jimmy Dean Division, financially evaluating new products. After Sara Lee Corp., my career spanned from Haagen Dazs to the Weather Channel. At Haagen Dazs, I was the finance manager for the South-Central Region, which was a sales & distribution region that included Georgia, Florida, Illinois, North Carolina, and South Carolina. At the Weather Channel, I was financially responsible for the Advertising Sales division. The experience I gained in corporate finance provides my students with a realistic view of what they will encounter after graduation.

ACTIVITY #1: ━━━━━━━━━━━━━━━━━━━━━━

The "strengths" that I utilized to fund my college education were athletics, academics, and financial need. What are your "strengths?" What are you good at? What can you use to help fund your college education? List five strengths below:

1. _____

2. _____

3. _____

4. _____

5. _____

Chapter 2

PLAN FOR IT

As a researcher in personal finance, I have seen evidence that individuals who plan are financially better off than those who don't plan. That is especially true in the case of paying for your college education. Most people don't have money to pay for a college education out of their own pocket. So, your goal should be to find a way to finance your education without taking out student loans. There is enough free money available for college, but you must plan.

As a finance professor, I make most decisions based on a cost/benefit analysis. In other words, I try to find the option that produces the greatest benefits and costs the least. To achieve this objective while funding your college education, you must think outside the box. The following example highlighting my niece's situation perfectly illustrates this.

Example #1: My Niece's Story
Recently, my niece decided she wanted to become a nurse and asked for my help. She was nervous because she had been out of high school for over ten years, and she was adamant about not taking out student loans to pay for her education. I told her that it could be done without loans if we planned and were aggressive in searching and applying for scholarships, grants, and fellowships.

We knew that Indiana University (IU) had a great nursing school, but my niece did her homework and found out that Ivy Tech had a two-year nursing program that served as a feeder program into IU's nursing school. IU's tuition is about three times greater than Ivy Tech's tuition, so the first part of our plan was for her to attend Ivy Tech for the first two years and then transfer to IU for her last two years. She applied and was admitted to several schools, but she stuck to the plan. We applied for as many grants and scholarships as possible.

She was awarded enough grant money to cover her tuition and fees, as well as her books, with a small refund leftover. Most importantly, she did not have to rely on any student loans at all. We will go through the same exercise of searching for scholarships and grants when she is ready to transfer to IU's nursing school.

ACTIVITY #2: ━━━━━━━━━━━━━━━━━━

Now think outside the box. What are some inexpensive options for you to fund your college education? Please list five.

1. _____

2. _____

3. _____

4. _____

5. _____

Your College Choice:

Everyone's college experience is different, and it is important to choose the college that best fits you. Some students would flourish at a large university, easily getting involved in campus life. While others might struggle at a large university but may flourish at a small college/university.

You certainly want to attend a college that's known for your desired major. For example, if you are from Indiana and you're thinking about a career in engineering or computer science, you would more than likely choose Purdue University, since it is known for its technology majors. If you're from Georgia and you are interested in technology majors, you would more than likely choose Georgia Institute of Technology. Both Purdue and Georgia Tech are public universities, meaning that they are supported by the state.

If you want to major in business and you're from Indiana, Indiana University (IU) is known for its business school, especially for its MBA program. If you are interested in becoming a writer or interested in journalism, the University of Georgia has one of the best journalism schools around. Before you apply to any college, research the best colleges/universities within your desired field. The US News & World report provides a national ranking called "Best Colleges".

Why Not an HBCU?

I believe that Historically Black Colleges and Universities (HBCU) have always been the preferred educational institution for many African Americans. In fact, prior to, during and for some time after the civil war (1861-1865), HBCUs were the only option for African Americans to receive a college education (HBCU First, 2022). Before the civil war, African Americans were prohibited from getting a college education in most southern states and discouraged from getting it in many northern states (HBCU First, 2022).

Cheyney University of Pennsylvania (1837) was the first HBCU, and for a long time after its inception, the only educational institution, to provide African Americans with a college degree specifically to become teachers (HBCU First, 2022). About fifteen years later, three other HBCUs were founded. The University of the District of Columbia was founded in 1851, followed by Lincoln University in 1854 and Wilberforce in 1856 (HBCU First, 2022).

In the south, Shaw College was founded in 1865 in North Carolina (HBCU First, 2022). Atlanta University was also founded in 1865 and was the first HBCU to offer graduate degrees to African Americans (HBCU First, 2022). Atlanta University is now Clark Atlanta University due to a consolidation in 1988 with Clark College (1869) (AUCC, 2022). In Atlanta Georgia, Morehouse College was founded in 1867 specifically for African American men and Spelman College was founded in 1881, specifically for African American women. Clark Atlanta University, Morehouse College and Spelman College are located next to each other, and they make up the Atlanta University Center (AUCC, 2022).

In 1862, the federal government's Morrill Land Grant Act provided land for states to establish colleges and universities to benefit the agricultural and mechanical arts (HBCU First, 2022). But 17 southern states demanded that their land grant colleges/universities be segregated and denied African Americans admissions to these land grant colleges/universities. Therefore in 1890, the federal government established a Second Morrill Act requiring states to establish a separate land grant college for African Americans (HBCU First, 2022). From this second Morrill Act, 19 HBCUs, which are land grant public colleges/universities were founded. These 19 HBCUs included Alabama A&M, Florida A&M, Tuskegee University, Central State University, Tennessee State University, etc. (HBCU First, 2022).

A couple of years ago, someone asked me if HBCUs were still relevant. And my answer was and always will be a resounding yes. Although African Americans now have many colleges/universities to choose from, HBCUs provides its students with a campus environment that fosters success. According to the United Negro College Fund, environment fit is important to success. In fact, African Americans feel more at home and perform better in colleges where they feel supported and safe (Lomax, 2022). According to a Gallup-USA Funds Minority College Graduates Report, African American graduates of HBCUs are more likely to be thriving and progressing in several areas of their lives, specifically in purpose and financial well-being, than African American graduates from other colleges (Seymour & Ray, 2015).

For me, Clark Atlanta University provided that safe space, and built my confidence in the most extraordinary way, and I didn't see it coming. I've always been a pretty good student and I've made good grades for the most part. But I did not like talking or participating in class. I certainly didn't like answering questions, even if I knew the answers. School and my grades were extremely important to me, but I was extremely shy.

Well, in my first finance class, the professor informed us that 50% of our grade was participation. This meant I had to talk and participate in class. So, I was determined to participate and get an A in the class. Well, after a couple of times of answering questions correctly, my confidence grew, and I became comfortable participating in class and became the go-to person for finance. In fact, in my second year of the MBA program, I was voted "Ms. Finance" by my peers. HBCUs are vital for the African American community, vital for the US and vital for the world.

ACTIVITY #3: ━━━━━━━━━━━━

Based on your preferred career, research the top schools. For example, if you want to be an engineer or be in business, which schools are the top schools for engineering or for business?

Career_____
1.

2.

3.

4.

5.

Career_____
1.

2.

3.

4.

5.

Career_____
1.

2.

3.

4.

5.

How Much Will It Cost?

How much will your dream college cost? This cost will most likely include tuition and fees to attend classes as well as room and board if you live on campus. Some colleges require that students live on campus for the first year or two. Juniors, seniors, and graduate students typically can live off campus in apartments. As such, these upperclassmen would have to pay rent, utilities, food, transportation to and from campus, and other expenses associated with living off campus.

In most states, aspiring students can choose between attending a public or private higher education institution. Public universities/colleges are owned and supported by the state. Therefore, they receive funding from the state that offsets the cost of tuition for students who are residents of that state.

Private universities/colleges typically do not receive state funding, so they typically depend on contributions and donations from alumni, private individuals, and corporations. As such, the tuition charged at private universities/colleges is usually more expensive than the in-state tuition charged at public universities. Public universities typically charge in-state tuition for its residence, and out-of-state tuition for non-residences.

College students who attend a public university/college in their home state not only pay cheaper tuition but also, qualify for any incentives the state offers to encourage its residents to stay in state for college. For example, Georgia offers the Hope Scholarship exclusively for its residents.

Below is a breakdown of the costs associated with attending a public university, based on the different in-state and out-of-state tuition rates.

PUBLIC UNIVERSITY	RESIDENT	NON-RESIDENT
Tuition	$9,790	$28,830
Fees	$1,390	$1,390
Books and Supplies	$888	$888
Room & Board	$10,904	$10,904
Transportation	$1,278	$2,112
Misc. Living Expenses	$3,292	$3,292
Total	$27,542	$47,416

Source: University of Georgia 2022-2023 Estimated Cost

Private universities/colleges charge one cost for all students. There is no distinction between in state or out-of-state tuition. For example, the cost breakdown to attend a private university is presented below.

PRIVATE UNIVERSITY	COST
Tuition	$28,450
Fees	$466
Room & Board	$9,300
Meal Plan	$5,378
Books and Supplies	$1,360
Transportation	$1,000
Personal Expenses	$2,160
Total Cost	$48,114

Source: Howard University 2021-2022 Estimated Cost

ACTIVITY #4

Now, do your homework and determine what your college education will cost based on your top three college choices by filling in the tables below.

UNIVERSITY #1	COST
Tuition	
Fees	
Books and Supplies	
Room & Board	
Transportation	
Misc. Living Expenses	
Total	

UNIVERSITY #2	COST
Tuition	
Fees	
Books and Supplies	
Room & Board	
Transportation	
Misc. Living Expenses	
Total	

UNIVERSITY #3	COST
Tuition	
Fees	
Books and Supplies	
Room & Board	
Transportation	
Misc. Living Expenses	
Total	

Chapter 3

SCHOLARSHIPS & GRANTS

If you intend to go to college, you should develop a game plan for how to pay for it in advance. If you or your family can afford to pay for your college education, out of your own pocket, you are the exception, and this book is probably not for you. However, if you are like most of us who can't afford to pay for college out of our own pocket, you are in the right place. You must do your homework on the options available for obtaining financial support that, unlike student loans, you do not have to pay back.

Everyone applying for federal funds for college must submit a Free Application for Federal Student Aid form or FAFSA form. Your potential colleges use your FAFSA information to determine your financial aid eligibility. Your financial need is the difference between the "Cost of Attendance" and your "Expected Family Contribution" (Financial Student Aid, 2022a).

Your "Expected Family Contribution" is an index, based on the information provided in the FAFSA form, and indicates the expected amount that you and/or your family can contribute towards your education (Financial Student Aid, 2022a). Your financial need will determine how much need-based aid you will receive (Financial Student Aid, 2022a). The deadline to submit your FAFSA may vary by college, but you should submit it as early as possible (Financial Student Aid, 2022a).

Scholarships are a great way to pay for a college education because these funds are free to you. However, competition for scholarships is fierce. Therefore, you need to be creative and hustle to find as many scholarships as possible for which you are eligible.

As you begin your search for scholarships, you first need to understand the difference between *Merit-based scholarships* and *Need-based scholarships*. *Merit-based scholarships* are awarded based on academic performance or academic performance plus a special talent. *Need-based scholarships* are granted according to the financial need of the student, typically determined by your FAFSA information (Federal Student Aid, 2022b). Applicants who qualify for both *Merit-based* and *Need-based* financial awards have more opportunities to receive scholarship funding.

Private Scholarships:

Private scholarships are typically awarded based on specific criteria. For example, the National Society of Black Engineers may offer scholarships for African American students majoring in engineering; or STEM organizations may offer scholarships for girls pursuing careers in the field of Science, Technology, Engineering, or Mathematics. Typically, there is a GPA requirement to qualify for these scholarships as well.

There are several scholarships out there, but a couple of the highly sought-after private scholarships are:

- The *Gates Scholarship*: Awarded annually to approx. 300 minority high school seniors who exhibit strong leadership skills, have a strong academic record, and have an exceptional financial need. A GPA of at least 3.3 plus eligibility for the Federal Pell Grant is usually required (Murtagh, 2018).

- *Coca Cola Scholarship Program*: An achievement-based scholarship for high school seniors that recognizes the student's ability to lead and serve and to make a commitment to their school and community. Each year, awards are $20,000 per person to 150 students based on academic merit and leadership skills (Murtagh, 2018).

- *Society of Women Engineers Scholarship*: Scholarships that support women interested in a career in engineering, engineering technology and computer science (Murtagh, 2018).

- *Google Scholarships*: Google aims to provide financial support to students, especially students from underserved minority communities, who aspire to pursue a career in technology (Murtagh, 2018).

- *Dell Scholars:* Dell Scholars are awarded $20,000, given a laptop, and assistance with textbooks. These students must be from an underserved and lower income household to achieve their dream of a college career (Murtagh, 2018).

- *United Negro College Fund (UNCF):* UNCF is the nation's largest provider of private scholarships to minority students. UNCF has raised over $4.7 billion to provide operating funds for 37 HBCUs and provides approx. 60,000 scholarships, annually, to college students (Murtagh, 2018).

State-Based Scholarships:

Each state offers scholarships as an incentive for high schoolers to stay in state and go to college. This coupled with the fact that students who stay at home, pay less expensive tuition makes it attractive to stay at home and go to college. For example, the state of Georgia offers the HOPE Scholarship Program for its residents which is highlighted below.

The *HOPE Scholarship Program* consists of the *HOPE Scholarship* which is a Merit-based scholarship for Georgia residents who demonstrate exceptional academic performance. Eligible high schoolers must at least have a 3.0 GPA or above for this scholarship (Georgia Student Finance Commission, 2022).

The *Zell Miller Scholarship* is also under the HOPE Scholarship Program. The *Zell Miller Scholarship* is also Merit-based but awards more money than the *HOPE Scholarship*. To be eligible, students must have a 3.7 GPA, SAT score of at least 1200 on reading and math portions, and an ACT score of at least 26. Students must maintain a 3.3 GPA while in college (Georgia Student Finance Commission, 2022). Most states provide some sort of scholarships for their residence.

ACTIVITY #5

Research any scholarships provided by your state and list five of these scholarships below that might apply to you.

1. _____

2. _____

3. _____

4. _____

5. _____

Scholarships at the University Level:

You should begin your search for scholarship opportunities on the website of the college you want to attend. Universities and colleges compile scholarships that are pertinent to their student body. In essence, these universities have done a scholarship search for you. You just have to apply for the scholarships. A sample listing of scholarships is illustrated below.

SCHOLARSHIPS
Gates Scholarship
Delaware Department of Education
United Negro College Fund
Pennsylvania Higher Education
Daniels Scholarship
Maryland Higher Education Commission
DC College Access Program
AmeriCorps
Gilman Scholarship
Vermont State Grant

Source: Howard University Website

Example #2: My Boss's Boss Daughter

A few years after I graduated from Indiana University, I was working at Indiana Bell in Indianapolis, IN. My boss' boss asked for my advice on paying for his daughter's college education. His daughter had been admitted to Brown University, an Ivy League school in Providence, Rhode Island.

I told him to purchase a scholarship book and have his daughter apply for every scholarship she may qualify for. These scholarships can be based on her grades, hobbies, the city, and state in which she lives, and any other personal talents or experiences.

After his daughter applied for the first few scholarships, she realized that most sought the same type of information and had similar essay requirements, which made the application process much easier. In the end, she was awarded a variety of different types of scholarships, such as a scholarship from the Chicago Piano Players because she played the piano and academic scholarships because she was a great student.

Through these scholarship awards, his daughter received enough financial support to pay for her tuition, fees, room, and board, leaving only her textbooks to be paid for by her father.

Example #3: An Innovative Student
Lena Harper (not her real name) was a marketing student at CAU several years ago. Lena was a member of the Financial Literacy Program as well, so her money management skills were good. Her talent was her ability to present a persuasive sales pitch. So, she entered sales pitch competitions where winners could win prize money.

She won enough prize money through these sales pitch competitions, to pay off all her student loans before she graduated. She was even able to pay off a loan that her mother had taken out to help her pay for her freshman year of college.

ACTIVITY #6: ▬▬▬▬▬▬▬▬▬▬▬▬

Look on the website of your top 3 preferred schools and list all scholarships that may apply to you.

University #1 Name_____

1.

2.

3.

4.

5.

University #2 Name_____

1.

2.

3.

4.

5.

University #3 Name_____

1.

2.

3.

4.

5.

Scholarships at the School Level:

The scholarship list on the university/college website most likely includes scholarships at the university level, meaning they apply to all students. However, scholarships and grants are also available at the school level. For example, the School of Business may offer scholarships to marketing or accounting students, or the School of Arts and Sciences may make scholarships available for chemistry or biology students.

These scholarships may or may not be advertised on the school's website, so you should contact the dean's office of that school to learn about these opportunities. Also, most universities have a Graduate School that oversees all graduate students. They, too, usually provide scholarships, grants, and/or assistantships for graduate students.

For example, when I was getting my PhD, I received an assistantship from my school as well as from the Graduate School. The assistantship from the Graduate School was for minority students pursuing their PhD. Below is a sample listing of scholarships from a business school.

SCHOLARSHIPS
NABA Future Leadership Scholarships (National Association of Black Accountants)
Bank of America
Jim Mann Family Scholarships
Be an Actuary Scholarship
The Hobbs Group
CIREI Scholarship
Mortgage Bankers Association Scholarship
Hickman Scholarship Program
John T. Lockton Scholarship
RIMS Spencer Scholarship

Source: University of Georgia's Terry School of Business Website

Scholars Programs:

Recently, corporations have set up "Scholars Programs" on college campuses to expose students to their company, especially companies in unique industries. Most scholar programs include internships for the scholars, tuition scholarships for the scholars and a mentorship program where scholars interact with professionals from the company. Oftentimes, scholarships can range from $1,000 up to full tuition scholarships for the year. Corporations prefer to start these programs early in a student's college career so that their scholars could come back and talk about their great experiences to fellow students on campus.

Scholar programs are used when companies have a difficult time recruiting a certain type of student and want to expose these students to a unique industry. For example, there are not many African American professionals within the Venture Capital industry. Venture Capital firms provide financing and funding for startup companies. A Venture Capital company might want to set up a scholar program to expose African American students to that industry and recruit them to their company.

ACTIVITY #7

Go to the website for the school within the university/college of your top three choices and examine the list of scholarships. If this information is not on the website, contact the dean's office directly. List five of these scholarships below for your top schools.

University #1_____

    1.

    2.

    3.

    4.

    5.

University #2_____

    1.

    2.

    3.

    4.

    5.

University #3_____

    1.

    2.

    3.

    4.

    5.

Athletic Scholarships:

As a child growing up in Indianapolis, Indiana, if I was not in school, I would play some type of sport all year long. In middle school and high school, I played volleyball, basketball, ran track in the spring, and played softball in the summer. Sports kept me out of trouble and over time I became a pretty good athlete, especially on the basketball court, playing the game I loved.

Being an athlete enabled me to get a basketball scholarship, and I played college basketball for two years before solely concentrating on my academics. At that point, I transitioned from relying on basketball scholarships to pay for my education to relying on grants to pay for my last few years as an undergraduate. Athletic scholarships, for many students, make earning a degree financially possible.

After playing basketball, my logical next step was to coach girls' basketball. I coached a girls' Amateur Athletic Union (AAU) basketball team, and this Nike travel team was known on the summer basketball circuit. Giving athletes exposure to college coaches and potential athletic scholarships was what I enjoyed about my coaching experience.

Even more gratifying was seeing so many young ladies go to college on basketball scholarships, as more than 97% of the Nike team's players received athletic scholarships. Despite their love of the game, I always cautioned my players to "Be a college student who happens to play basketball, don't be a basketball player who happens to go to college." In other words, take full advantage of the opportunity your athletic talent and experience has given you, which is a free college education, by focusing on your studies.

41

Example #4: Basketball Player

My greatest success as a basketball coach involved one of my athletes who wanted to study nursing and play basketball at a particular university because her mother had attended this university. The problem was that this university was not recruiting her. I told her she needed to recruit them; contact them, send them a video, and let them know who she was.

She did exactly that, and a few weeks later, I received a call from one of the coaches of the women's basketball program. We had a great conversation about this athlete. I told the coach that this student was a really good player with a great shot and that she was smart, evidenced by her high GPA and SAT scores. More importantly, I informed the coach that this was a good kid who would be a leader in her program.

This student received a basketball scholarship from this university and took to heart my advice about being a college student first and a basketball player second. She graduated in 2015 with a bachelor's degree in Registered Nursing and went on to earn her master's degree in Registered Nursing again from the same university in 2018.

Since graduating, she has been working as a Women's Health and Nursing Practitioner for the hospital affiliated with this university, and she is now enrolled in their Nursing Practice Doctoral Program. Employees of this hospital can go to this university for free. This young lady is on track to receive her third degree from this university, and it all started with an athletic scholarship. All three degrees were paid for through scholarships, grants, and fellowships.

Internet Search for Scholarships:

After applying for the scholarships that you found on the university/college website and at the school level, next turn to the internet. You should first do a search, on any browser, for scholarships that would pertain to you. For example, if you are a student returning to college to finish your degree, search for scholarships for *returning students*. Next, set up an account on a scholarship search website and look for more opportunities that may be available to you. Some of the popular search sites are:

- scholarships.com
- fastweb.com
- collegescholarships.org
- niche.com
- scholarships360.org

(Lutli, 2021)

The US Department of Labor, Employment and Training Administration also offers a free scholarship search tool under *Careeronestop.org*. The steps for getting to this search tool is as follows:

1.) Go to Careeronestop.org
2.) Under "Find Training"
3.) Go to "Pay for Training"
4.) Select "Scholarships"
5.) Click on "Scholarship Finder"

Under this scholarship engine, you can search for scholarships by level of study, award type, where you live, what you will study, your affiliation and your gender. You should do a thorough search of the 8,000 scholarships available through this website.

ACTIVITY #8:

Search for scholarships on the scholarship search engine of your choice and list at least five scholarships that you can apply for below. Pay particular attention to scholarships that align with your strengths.

1. _____

2. _____

3. _____

4. _____

5. _____

What About Grants?

The most popular federal grant that students can receive to help defray the cost of their college education is the Pell Grant. The federal government provides Pell Grants to undergraduate students who display exceptional financial need (Financial Student Aid, 2022b).

Your determined financial need depends on your expected family contribution, the cost of attendance (determined by your school), your status as a full-time or part-time student, and whether you plan to attend a full academic year or less. Your eligibility for the Pell Grant is determined through your FAFSA application (Financial Student Aid, 2022b).

Aside from the Pell Grant, the federal government also offers the Federal Supplemental Educational Opportunity Grant (FSEOG) which is awarded to between 100 - 4,000 undergraduates who have demonstrated exceptional financial need. In addition to these, the TEACH grant is awarded to those students interested in the teaching profession (Financial Student Aid, 2022b). There are also state grants available through your state.

Your Last Option - Student Loans:

Nowadays, students are graduating with an enormous amount of student loan debt. According to Student Loan Hero, in 2019, 69% of students took out student loans, with an average balance of $29,900. Moreover, 14% of their parents took out $37,200 in student loans, through the Parent Loan for Undergraduate Students (Parent PLUS) program (Kantrowitz, 2020).

Student loans should be used only when absolutely necessary or as a last resort. If you must use student loans to pay for your education, take out only what you need. If you take out only what you need, you will likely not receive a large refund after the college processes your loan and applies the necessary funding to pay your tuition, fees, and room & board.

However, a refund of a couple hundred dollars should suffice. Just because the university awards you a student loan, does not mean that you must accept it. You can decline any student loans offered. Again, your goal should be to fund your college education without student loans because they must be paid back when you graduate.

If you must take out a student loan, be sure to choose student loans that are the least expensive which would be those loans with the lowest interest rate. Also, a *direct subsidized loan* is preferable to a *direct unsubsidized loan*. The U.S. Department of Education pays the interest on *direct subsidized loans* while the student is in school and during the grace period or deferment period (Financial Student Aid, 2022b).

On the other hand, the government does not pay the interest on *direct unsubsidized student loans*. The borrower is responsible for paying back the full amount of the loan plus interest. This interest starts accruing when the loan payments are dispersed and while the student is in school. Financial need is not required to qualify for a direct unsubsidized loan. Financially, direct unsubsidized student loans are the least attractive option, between these two loans (Financial Student Aid, 2022b).

Student Loan Forgiveness:

If you find yourself with any amount of student loan debt, but certainly an overwhelming amount of student loan debt, you should explore ways to get those loans forgiven. The federal government offers various ways for you to qualify for student loan forgiveness.

First, it is important that you understand the various student loan payment plans offered by the federal government. The "Standard Payment Plan" spreads your account balance over 10 years, per an interest rate, and comes up with a monthly amount (Financial Student Aid, 2022b). You don't have to accept the "Standard Payment Plan". There are a total of eight different payment plans, some of which are sensitive to your income.

For example, there is the "Income Based Repayment Plan" where your payments would be 10% or 15% of your discretionary income, but never more than a standard payment (Financial Student Aid, 2022b). This plan is for individuals who have a high debt balance relative to their income. Any unpaid balance after 20 or 25 years of on time payments will be forgiven (Financial Student Aid, 2022b).

There are other payment plans where your payments start lower than the "Standard Repayment Plan" such as the "Graduated Repayment Plan". In the "Graduated Repayment Plan", the initial payments start out low and gradually increase typically every two years and will ensure that your loan will be paid off within 10 years (Financial Student Aid, 2022b). Go to the US Department of Education website and find the payment plan for you.

The federal government offers some programs to forgive student loans. For example, the "Teacher Loan Program" forgives loans for people who teach full time for five consecutive years in certain elementary and/or secondary schools or work for an educational service agency that serves low-income families (Financial Student Aid, 2022b).

President Joseph Biden, our 46th president, is making a concerted effort to forgive student loans. Recently, the Biden-Harris administration offered the Student Debt Relief plan. In this plan families and individuals making less than $125,000 can get up to $20,000 in student loan debt forgiven (Financial Student Aid, 2022c). The federal government also revamped a program called PSLF (Public Service Loan Forgiveness), which has been around for a long time, but it was not effectively working. This program was revamped so now individuals working for the government or working for a not-for-profit organization or in the public sector can get their loans forgiven after 10 years of paying their student loans on time (Financial Student Aid, 2022b).

Through the *Nurses Education Student Repayment Program*, nurses are also getting their loans forgiven by the federal government. Also, those who work for AmeriCorps or in the military have special programs to forgive their student loans (Financial Student Aid, 2022b). States also sponsor student loan forgiveness programs.

ACTIVITY #9: ━━━━━━━━━━━━━━━

If you currently have student loans, research any program that may help you forgive these loans. List those programs below.

1. _____

2. _____

3. _____

4. _____

5. _____

Chapter 4

YOU ARE IN NOW

Once you have been admitted to the university/college of your choice, it is up to you to be a prudent steward of your finances. Effectively managing your money will take stress off you. But first, you have to choose your major.

Choosing Your Major:

Of course, you should major in an area that you are passionate about and that appeals to you. However, from a financial perspective, I always tell students to start with the end in mind when choosing a major. For example, if you want to be an accountant, a lawyer, or a psychologist, find out how much the average accountant, lawyer or psychologist earns. Then consider if the income (benefits) of that career justifies its cost.

To do this, you need to investigate the education required to become an accountant, a lawyer, or a psychologist, and the cost of that education. For example, you can become an accountant by majoring in accounting, typically within the School of Business, and earning a bachelor's degree. But for you to really advance in an accounting career, you must become a Certified Public Accountant (CPA). Therefore, you should get a master's degree typically in accounting (MA), which requires an additional year of schooling.

To be a lawyer, you need a bachelor's degree, perhaps in pre-law, but typically in any major. Then you must complete law school, which is an additional four years of school. To be a psychologist, you must have a bachelor's degree, typically majoring in psychology within the School of Arts and Science. You also need a master's degree and a doctorate. These requirements amount to an additional six years of school.

Once you are aware of the average salary and the costs involved in preparing for the career you are considering, you should perform a cost/benefit analysis. Ideally, the analysis will show that any additional costs will generate more salary in your career.

In the graph below, the major that looks to be the best investment is in computer science. A computer science degree only costs $18,320, but with that degree, a person can potentially earn a starting salary of $61,321 per year. The least attractive investment, according to the graph below, is education. The cost of a degree in education is $18,589, while the potential starting salary is only $34,891.

MAJOR COST/BENEFIT

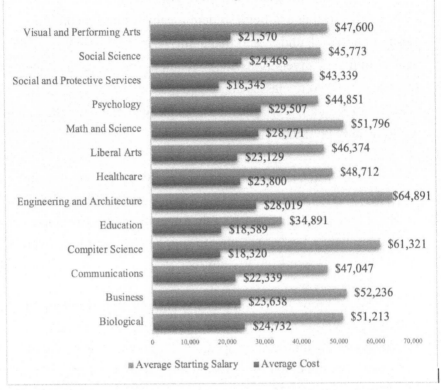

Visual and Performing Arts — $21,570 / $47,600
Social Science — $24,468 / $45,773
Social and Protective Services — $18,345 / $43,339
Psychology — $29,507 / $44,851
Math and Science — $28,771 / $51,796
Liberal Arts — $23,129 / $46,374
Healthcare — $23,800 / $48,712
Engineering and Architecture — $28,019 / $64,891
Education — $18,589 / $34,891
Compiter Science — $18,320 / $61,321
Communications — $22,339 / $47,047
Business — $23,638 / $52,236
Biological — $24,732 / $51,213

■ Average Starting Salary   ■ Average Cost

Source: Sallie Mae

53

Budgeting in College:

College is the place you go to grow up and learn to manage your money. Being a college student means waking up on time, doing your own laundry, and managing your own money. When I was at Indiana University, living on campus, my job as a college student was to go to classes and make good grades. My tuition, fees, room & board were paid for through financial aid dollars, and I was usually on the meal plan.

I received a small refund check at the beginning of each semester, and my family would send me about $80 every two weeks. I typically held a work study job at the university library or bookstore, where I earned money to supplement what I received in the refund check and from my family.

When I moved off campus and had my own apartment, I had more expenses to manage. I had to pay for rent, utilities, transportation to and from campus, etc. I also had to ensure that I had books and materials for class and money for food and other necessities. This was certainly a microcosm of what I experienced after I graduated and entered Corporate America.

Example #5: My Student

This example highlights that college is where you go to grow up. You should also develop the skills necessary to successfully live independently. In this example, a student's parents used college to teach their son valuable life lessons.

About four years ago, this young man, Christopher (not his real name), who was a graduating senior at CAU from the Washington DC area, was enrolled in my retirement class.

Christopher's parents were successful professionals in the DC area. Because of his parent's financial information, Christopher was not eligible for any financial aid to pay for college.

Christopher's father had informed him that he had to find a way to pay for his own college education and he could not depend on student loans. His father promised to keep health insurance in place for Christopher while he was in school, but that was it.

While Christopher was in college, he worked as a general contractor, hiring subcontractors to renovate kitchens and bathrooms in people's homes. He used the income from being a general contractor to pay for his college tuition and fees and to pay for his living expenses. As a result, Christopher graduated free from student loan debt.

A Written Budget:

To properly manage your money, you should maintain a written budget, per month, per semester, and then an overall budget for the year while you are in college. If you are living on campus, the university will usually apply your financial aid to the cost of your tuition, fees, room & board, and a typical meal plan.

Each semester you will typically receive a refund check, which you can use to purchase any books or supplies you need for your classes. Colleges and universities today offer book bundles that allow you to pay one set fee for all your books, and this fee is usually taken out of your financial aid before you receive a refund. If you have any money left from your refund check, deposit it into your checking account.

Below is an example of a student financial aid award with cost. In the example, the total financial aid the student receives for the semester is $16,800 per semester or $33,600 per year. The total school cost for the semester is $14,151, which includes $4,643 for tuition and fees, $7,796 for room & board, and $1,712 for other expenses. When the total cost of $14,151 is subtracted from the financial aid for the student totaling $16,800, this leaves the student with a $2,649 refund for the semester or $5,298 per year.

ABC UNIVERSITY	_Fall Semester_	_Spring Semester_
Cost:		
Tuition & Fees	$4,643	$4,643
Room & Board	$7,796	$7,796
Other Expenses	$1,712	$1,712
Total Cost	**$14,151**	**$14,151**
Financial Aid Description:		
Federal PELL Grant	$3,247	$3,247
Federal Supplemental Grant	$500	$500
Foundation Scholarship	$6,500	$6,500
Dean's Scholarship	$5,253	$5,253
Talent Incentive Grant	$1,300	$1,300
Total	**$16,800**	**$16,800**
Refund	**$2,649**	**$2,649**

That refund of $2,649 per semester, $5,298 per year, is considered income for the semester. This income should be put in your written budget which is illustrated below. When added to the student's $750 monthly wages from employment and the $125 contribution from their family, the total the student has in income for August is $2,774 and for January is $3,524. Every month besides August and January the student will have income between $750 and $875.

ABC University	August	September	October	November	December	January	February	March	April	May
Income										
Refund	2,649					2,649				
Wages		750	750	750	750	750	750	750	750	750
Family	125	125	0	125	0	125	0	125	0	125
Total Income	2,774	875	750	875	750	3,524	750	875	750	875
Expenses										
Books	650					650				
Car	600	600	600	600	600	600	600	600	600	600
Gas	150	150	150	150	150	150	150	150	150	150
Cell Phone	75	75	75	75	75	75	75	75	75	75
Misc	120	120	120	120	120	120	120	120	120	120
Weekend	100	100	100	100	100	100	100	100	100	100
Total Expenses	1,695	1,045	1,045	1,045	1,045	1,695	1,045	1,045	1,045	1,045
Mo. Balance	1,079	(170)	(295)	(170)	(295)	1,829	(295)	(170)	(295)	(170)
Total Balance	1,079	909	614	444	149	1,978	1,683	1,513	1,218	1,048

In terms of expenses, at the beginning of the Fall and Spring semester, or in August and January, the student pays a total of $1,695. This includes $650 for books/material, and the rest of the expenses include a car payment, gas, cell phone, weekend expenses and miscellaneous expenses. The total expense for every other month, besides August and January is $1,045. These months don't include books/materials, but they include all other expenses.

The student should save their refund check and income, in their savings account to cover all their expenses for the semester and for the year. According to the budget above, the student should have $149 left in December at the end of the fall semester, and $1,048 left over in May at the end of the school year.

ACTIVITY #10: ━━━━━━━━━━━━━━━━━━━━━━━━━━━━━

There are plenty of budget tools out there for college students. The most popular ones include:

- Mint
- Every Dollar
- You need a budget
- Good Budget
- Digit
- Pocket Guard

Source: College Finance

Research each of these budget tools and determine the one that works for you.

Credit Cards:

I am often asked if college students should establish a positive credit history while in school. My answer is always the same. A college student should only worry about grades and gaining experience through internships while in school. Students do not need to establish credit while in college and, therefore, do not need credit cards.

You typically borrow money on a credit card because you don't have the cash now to pay for some expense, which is paid back later, with interest. College students typically don't have enough income to pay off a credit card every month or over time while they're in college. A debit card is sufficient for a college student to manage their money. Students should live on the money they currently have rather than living on money borrowed from the future. Mapping out a budget will help students live within their means without relying on credit cards.

Furthermore, being able to start your career with a clean slate in terms of credit (i.e., no negative items on the credit report) will greatly benefit you. One of the worst things that can happen to students, financially, is to run up high balances on a credit card and struggle to pay the bill, miss payments, and ruin their credit before you even graduate. Also, the financial stress of worrying about not being able to pay credit card bills can derail a student's performance in the classroom.

Credit card companies are willing to give students credit cards even if they don't have a job nor income. These companies are assuming that the student will graduate, get a job, and then have income to pay for a credit card. But students may be tempted to use the card while they're in college and run up a balance that they can't pay off.

I've often heard that credit card companies may also want to provide students with their first credit card because people usually keep their first credit card for many years. However, you must protect yourself and your financial future by resisting the temptation to use credit cards, thereby avoiding the risk of misusing them and ruining your credit.

Negotiate Your Salary:

An essential element of setting a positive course for your life after college is being prepared when negating your salary for your future employer. First, internships are essential for gaining valuable experience and for determining if the type of work performed is the type of work you want to do long term. You should also determine if the company that you intern with is a good fit for you.

In other words, internships provide a way for the company to interview the student, but they also provide a way for the student to interview the company. During your senior year, once you have interviewed with several companies and you have secured an offer, or multiple offers, do your homework so that you negotiate the best potential salary. To gain information to make a sound decision on an offer, first go to www.salarywizard.com and determine the average salary for the job you are considering, in the city where you will be working. For example, if you are offered a position as a financial analyst in Chicago, Illinois, determine the average salary for a financial analyst in that city.

In the diagram below, the average salary for a financial analyst, with a bachelor's degree, with less than one year of experience is $63,102. Compare this average salary to your current offer and negotiate if the offer is too low. If you are in the top 10% of your class, your projected salary should be $75,520.

(Source: www.salarywizard.com)

Also, research the employee benefits that the company offers, such as retirement plans, stock bonus plans, paid time off, and relocation packages. This can also help you decide where you want to work.

ACTIVITY #11: ━━━━━━━━━━━━━━━━━━━━━━━

Pull the average salary of whatever jobs you hope to obtain once you graduate in the city you plan to live in and list them below. If you have an offer in hand, compare that offer to the information below.

1. _____

2. _____

3. _____

4. _____

5. _____

CONCLUSION

This book should financially guide you into and through college. Ideally, you should purchase this book while you're in middle school or high school, so you have plenty of time to plan for your college career. It is up to you to plan and aggressively search for scholarships and grants to pay for college. Today, there are so many organizations, companies and individuals offering scholarships, grants, and fellowships, you just have to search for them. After you've been awarded enough scholarships or grants to pay for your tuition, fees, and room & board, you have to manage your money in college.

A college student who has to worry about how they will pay their bills or how they will eat has unwanted financial stress. That's why it is so important for you to effectively manage your money while in college. It's also important to be prepared for your career after college. In the end, my sincere hope for you is that you successfully graduate with your college degree with little to no debt. If that happens, my job is done.

DEFINITIONS

Book Bundle – Course material packaged together for purchase. Typically, the student pays one fee for this bundle and this fee is included in their cost of attending college.

Feeder Program – A program where its students start at one program and then enter another specific program at the end of the first program.

In-State Tuition – The cost of a state resident to attend college in their own state.

Mythology – A set of legends, stories, or beliefs especially ones that have a religious or cultural tradition.

Out of State Tuition – The tuition rate students pay when attending a public university out of their state of resident.

Parent Plus Loan – Loans made by the Department of Education to parents of dependent undergraduate students for the benefit of their child who is the student.

Private University – A college or university that operates as an educational non-profit organization and does not receive its primary funding from that state government.

Public University – A university or college that is in state ownership or receives significant public funds through a national or subnational government.

Student Loan Forgiveness – Release from having to repay student loans in full or in part.

Venture Capital Companies – Companies that provide private equity funding to startup companies.

REFERENCES

AUCC (2022). *History. Historical Overview.* The Atlanta University Center Consortium. Atlanta, GA. Retrieved from: https://aucenter.edu/history/

Federal Student Aid (2022a). *Understanding Financial Aid. How Financial Aid Works.* U.S. Department of Education. Washington, DC. Retrieved from https://studentaid.gov/h/understand-aid/how-aid-works

Federal Student Aid (2022b). *Understanding Financial Aid. Types of Financial Aid.* U.S. Department of Education. Washington, DC. Retrieved from: https://studentaid.gov/understand-aid/types

Federal Student Aid (2022c). *The Biden-Harris Administration's Student Debt Relief Plan Explained.* U.S. Department of Education. Washington, DC. Retrieved from: https://studentaid.gov/debt-relief-announcement/

Georgia Student Finance Commission (2022). *HOPE. The Official Website of the State of Georgia.* Tucker, Georgia. Retrieved from: https://gsfc.georgia.gov/hope

HBCU First (2022). *The History of Historically Black Colleges and Universities.* HBCU First. New York, NY. Retrieved from https://hbcufirst.com/resources/hbcu-history-timeline

Kantrowitz, M. (2020). *Average students loan debt at graduation.* Saving for College. Miami, Florida. Retrieved from: https://www.savingforcollege.com/article/average-student-loan-debt-at-graduation

Lomax, M. L., (2022). *Six Reasons HBCUs Are More Important than ever.* United Negro College Fund (UNCF). Washington, DC. Retrieved from https://uncf.org/the-latest/6-reasons-hbcus-are-more-important-than-ever

Lutli. B. (2021). *Student Loans: The 9 best scholarship search engines.* BankRate. New York, NY. Retrieved from: https://www.bankrate.com/loans/student-loans/scholarship-search-engines/

Murtagh, A. (2018). *11 Private scholarships to help you pay for college.* US News and World Report. New York, NY. Retrieved from: https://www.usnews.com/education/best-colleges/paying-for-college/articles/2018-09-20/11-private-scholarships-to-help-you-pay-for-college

Seymour, S. & Ray, J. (2015). *Grads of Historically Black Colleges Have Well-Being Edge.* Gallup. Education. Washington, D.C. Retrieved from: https://news.gallup.com/poll/186362/grads-historically-black-colleges-edge.aspx

ABOUT THE AUTHOR

Dr. Crystal R. Hudson is the Department Chair of Accounting and Finance at Clark Atlanta University. Dr. Hudson also serves as the Director of CAU's Financial Planning program, a program that produces future Certified Financial Planners (CFPs). Dr. Hudson is an Associate Professor and has been at Clark Atlanta University for the past 10 years.

Dr. Hudson has a stellar research record focusing on African Americans' economic lives. Some of her publications include *"African American Financial Socialization"*, *"Investment Behavior: Factors that Impact African American Women's Investment Behavior"* and *"Wealth: Factors that Affect African American Wealth"*. Dr. Hudson has also co-authored the book *"Overcoming Obstacles-Experiences of Black Financial Services Professionals"*.

Prior to coming to CAU, Dr. Hudson had a successful career in Corporate Finance with such companies as The Weather Channel, Haagen Dazs and Sara Lee, Inc. Dr. Hudson earned a BS in Operations & Systems Management from Indiana University, MBA in Finance from Clark Atlanta University, and PhD in Financial Planning and Consumer Economics from the University of Georgia.

ABOUT THE EDITOR

Ms. Taylor J. Bridgeforth is a freelance editor, fiction writer, podcast host and group fitness instructor. Her first Young Adult novel will be published in October 2023. She lives in Indianapolis, IN.

Made in USA - Kendallville, IN
91211_9781940698229
12.20.2022 1333